THE WRITING BUG

by

Lee Bennett Hopkins

photographs by

Diane Rubinger

 Richard C. Owen Publishers, Inc.
Katonah, New York

Meet the Author titles

Verna Aardema *A Bookworm Who Hatched*

Eve Bunting *Once Upon a Time*

Lois Ehlert *Under My Nose*

Jean Fritz *Surprising Myself*

Paul Goble *Hau Kola Hello Friend*

Ruth Heller *Fine Lines*

Lee Bennett Hopkins *The Writing Bug*

James Howe *Playing with Words*

George Ella Lyon *A Wordful Child*

Margaret Mahy *My Mysterious World*

Karla Kuskin *Thoughts, Pictures, and Words*

Rafe Martin *A Storyteller's Story*

Patricia Polacco *Firetalking*

Cynthia Rylant *Best Wishes*

Jane Yolen *A Letter from Phoenix Farm*

Text copyright © 1993 by Lee Bennett Hopkins

Photographs copyright © 1993 by Diane Rubinger

Richard C. Owen Publishers, Inc.

P.O. Box 585

Katonah, New York 10536

Library of Congress Cataloging-in-Publication Data

Hopkins, Lee Bennett.
    The writing bug / by Lee Bennett Hopkins ; photographs by Diane Rubinger.
      p.   cm. — (Meet the author)
    Summary: Noted children's poet Lee Bennett Hopkins recounts his life and describes how his daily activities and writing process are interwoven.
    ISBN 1-878450-38-7 (hard)
    1 . Hopkins, Lee Bennett — Biography — Juvenile literature .
2 . Authors, American — 20th century — Biography — Juvenile literature .
3 . Authorship — Juvenile literature . [1. Hopkins, Lee Bennett.
2 . Authors, American.] I . Rubinger, Diane, ill . II . Title .
III . Series : Meet the author (Katonah, N . Y .)
PS3558.O63544Z466   1993
813 ' . 54 — dc20
[B]   93-11994

The text type was set in Caslon 540

Editor-in-Chief Janice Boland

Production Manager Amy J. Haggblom

Printed in the United States of America

9 8 7 6 5 4 3

To the Teacher, the Gardener,
and the Dude.

Dear Friends,

I never thought of becoming a writer.

It happened by accident.

I was stung by the writing bug the first time
an article I wrote appeared in a magazine.

I've been writing ever since.

I grew up in a single-parent household.
My mother struggled hard to take care of me
and my younger brother and sister
after my father left.

We lived in several apartments
before moving to a project development
in Newark, New Jersey.
Two of my novels, *Mama* and *Mama and Her Boys*,
are about my life as a young child
growing up in Newark.
I lived in the same project until I graduated from
Newark State Teachers College,
now called Kean College.

I began my career as a sixth-grade teacher
in Fair Lawn, New Jersey.
After having taught for many years,
I began writing articles for teachers
about the things I did with my students
to make learning more exciting.
Today, I do many different kinds of writing.
I write books for teachers and librarians.
I write picture books and novels,
and I write poetry.
There isn't a day that goes by
that I'm not reading poetry
or working on a poem of my own.

I begin my work day early in the morning.
After breakfast, I take Dude,
my Cavalier King Charles spaniel,
out for his morning walk.
Then I go upstairs to my study,
where most of my writing is done.

Dude stays downstairs.
Once in a while he comes upstairs
to visit me.
I pet and pat him.
Then he goes back downstairs to let me work.
He seems to know I am busy.

All of my writing is done in longhand in pencil.
When I'm happy with what I've written,
I type the finished piece on a typewriter.
I don't use a word processor or computer.
I suppose one day I will,
but now I'm too busy to spend the time needed
to learn how to use these machines!

My library is in my study.
It contains thousands of children's books
and my many files filled
with ideas for future books.
When I get tired of reading or writing
I glance up from my desk to behold the Hudson River,
which flows right outside my window.
Its beauty and majesty inspire me to write.

I get ideas from everywhere, it seems.
Sometimes a poem will sprout from remembering things
that happened to me while I was young—
like my poem:

       "This Tooth"
       I jiggled it
           jaggled it
           jerked it.
       I pushed
           pulled
           poked it.
       But—

       As soon as I stopped, and left it alone,
       This tooth came out on its very own!

Sometimes poems come from experiences
I have with Dude.
Once, when Dude was very young,
he had to spend two nights at the vet's office.
This experience led me to write:
"Overnight at the Vet's"

I found
a strand
of snow-white hair

strewn upon his
favorite chair

I wonder how
he's feeling there

alone—

I wonder
if he wants
his bone.

I wonder
if he'll catch
a flea—

I wonder
if
he
misses
me.

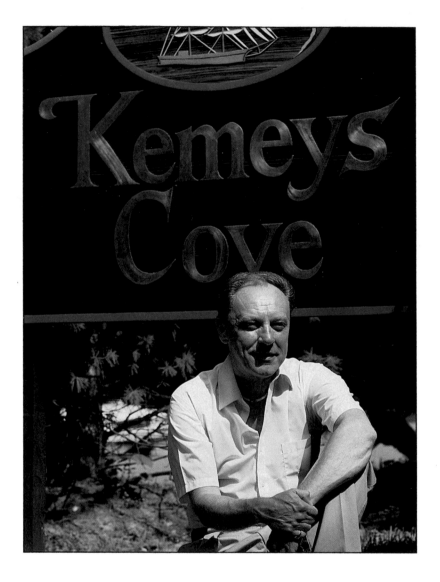

After living in or near cities all my life,
I moved to Kemeys Cove about twenty years ago.
Being a city child, I knew more about pigeons,
sidewalks, and sirens than I knew about

Canada geese,

scarecrows, or gardens.

I love living here at Kemeys Cove,
but I still love the bustling energy of the city.

The minute I get aboard the train to New York,
I feel a great sense of excitement,
knowing what lies ahead less than one hour away. . .
the people, the buildings,
the noise, the stores, the theatre.

When I leave it all behind and return home,
the quiet and magic of the country
take over my senses.

I love to see, hear, smell, and feel each season.
Spring with its green beginnings,
summer with its red-hot heat,
autumn in colors of gold and rust,
and winter with its gray-whiteness
are all special times for me.

Spring and summer are my favorite seasons.
I can go into the garden
where flowers burst with color,
where cucumbers and tomatoes grow.

Sometimes being in the garden will spark
an idea for a new poem.

Might I write about this rabbit statue,

this old painted and repainted red bench,

or this stream, where wriggly things tickle my toes,
and the coolness of the water seems
to make the summer heat disappear for a while?

Besides writing poetry,
I also put together collections of poetry,
called anthologies.
Most of the poems in my anthologies
are written by others, but sometimes
I include one or two of my own.
How do I begin?
First, I come up with an idea for a topic.
Then I search for all the poems
I can find on that subject.

I look through the hundreds of books
I have in my library
and I search for new books in bookstores.
I read and reread hundreds of poets' works,
whittling away until I've found
just the right poems for my anthology.

One anthology I worked on
for many years was *Side by Side*,
a collection filled with old and new rhymes.
If you look on page 80 of *Side by Side*,
you can see these drawings on the bottom of the page.
The left side shows me as a young boy
sitting in front of the house I was born in,
at 806 Philo Street, in Scranton, Pennsylvania.
On the right side is a drawing
of the artist, Hilary Knight,
in a scene where he grew up
in Roslyn, Long Island, New York.
Hilary Knight and I became good friends
while working on the book.

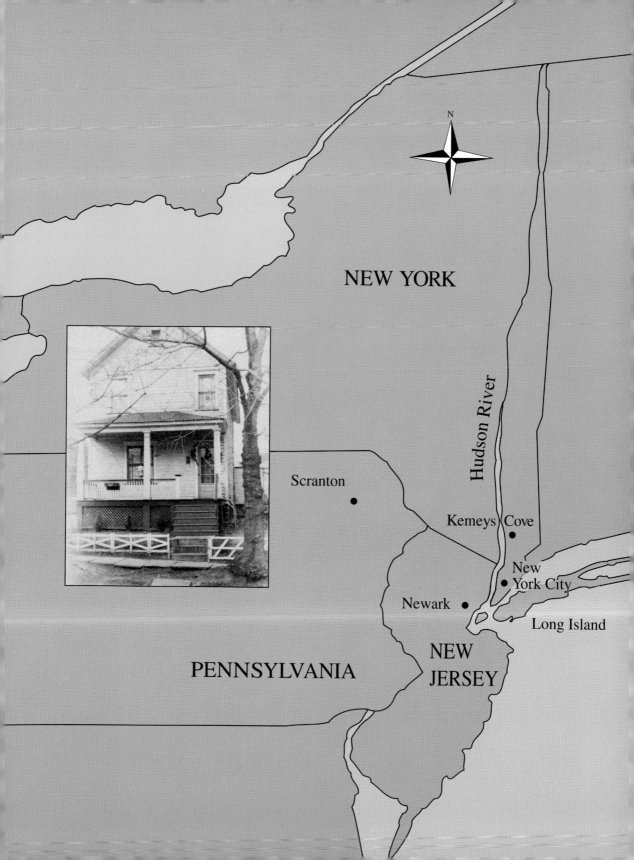

NEW YORK

Hudson River

Scranton

Kemeys Cove

New
York City

Newark

Long Island

PENNSYLVANIA

NEW
JERSEY

In 1985, I was chosen Children's Book Week Poet.
I wrote a poem for the celebration
called "Good Books, Good Times!"
It appeared on a bookmark which was sent
all over the United States,
with an illustration by Marc Brown.

GOOD BOOKS,
GOOD TIMES!

Good books.
Good times.
Good stories.
Good rhymes.
Good beginnings.
Good ends.
Good people.
Good friends.
Good fiction.
Good facts.
Good adventures.
Good acts.
Good stories.
Good rhymes.
Good books.
Good times.

© 1985 Lee Bennett Hopkins
Art by Marc Brown

I'm so glad I wrote this verse.
It's about my love of books
and my love of boys and girls—who read.
Yes, the writing bug stung.
The wound never healed,
and I hope it never, ever will.
May each and every one of you
have *good* books and *good* times
throughout *your* lives.
Happy Reading.
Happy Poetry-ing.
Your book friend,

Lee Bennett Hopkins

Other Books by Lee Bennett Hopkins

Creatures; *Dinosaurs*; *Flit, Flutter, Fly!*; *Happy Birthday*; *On the Farm*; *Questions*; *Rainbows are Made: Poems by Carl Sandburg*; *Side by Side*; *Surprises*; *Through Our Eyes*; *To the Zoo*; and many others.

About the Photographer

Diane Rubinger enjoys photographing adults and children. She lives fifty miles north of New York City in a village called Bedford. She especially enjoyed spending two sultry summer days near the Hudson River with Lee Bennett Hopkins and his dog, Dude.

Acknowledgments

Photographs on pages 4, 6, and 29 courtesy of Lee Bennett Hopkins. "This Tooth" copyright © 1974 by Lee Bennett Hopkins. "Overnight at the Vet's" copyright © 1992 by Lee Bennett Hopkins. "Good Books, Good Times!" copyright © 1985 by Lee Bennett Hopkins. Reprinted by permission of Curtis Brown, Ltd. Art copyright © 1985 by Marc Brown. Bookmark appears courtesy of Marc Brown. Illustration on page 17 from *On the Farm* by Lee Bennett Hopkins; illustrated by Laurel Molk. Text copyright © 1991 by Lee Bennett Hopkins; illustrations copyright © 1991 by Laurel Molk. By permission of Little, Brown and Company. Photograph on page 17 courtesy of Janice Boland. Photograph on page 18 courtesy of Richard C. Owen. Illustration on page 28 from *Side by Side: Poems to Read Together* collected by Lee Bennett Hopkins, illustrated by Hilary Knight © 1988. Reprinted by permission of the publisher, Simon & Schuster Books for Young Readers, New York.

CONCORDIA UNIVERSITY LIBRARY
2811 NE Holman St.
Portland, OR 97211-6099